AF211928

DYLAN EVERITT

HOW TO BORROW

The Comprehensive Guide on Finances and Loans, Learn Everything You Need to Know about Student Loans and Loan Consolidations to Finally Get Out of Debt

Descrierea CIP a Bibliotecii Naţionale a României
DYLAN EVERITT
    HOW TO BORROW. The Comprehensive Guide on
Finances and Loans, Learn Everything You Need to Know
about Student Loans and Loan Consolidations to Finally Get
Out of Debt / Dylan Everitt – Bucharest: Editura My Ebook, 2021
    ISBN

DYLAN EVERITT

HOW TO BORROW

The Comprehensive Guide on Finances and Loans, Learn Everything You Need to Know about Student Loans and Loan Consolidations to Finally Get Out of Debt

My Ebook Publishing House
Bucharest, 2021

CONTENTS

CONTENTS

INTRODUCTION

Almost nothing in life is free and loans are no different. Loans are basically a seemingly non complicated way of lending and borrowing but if one were to take the time to read the fine print, it could probably paint quite a scary picture. Get the help you need here.

CHAPTER 1

LOAN BASICS

Synopsis

A loan is an advancement of money or something of value with the promise or a bargain struck between the parties involved to redeem the full sum with interest within a stipulated period of time.

The Basics

The interest is usually calculated proportionate to the sum borrowed and paid back along with the principal in segment for an agreed amount of time.

The terms and interest amounts are usually not negotiable and in most cases are quite high. However it is still the most popular means of acquiring something legally and legitimately where payment is not immediately completely covered.

The general calculation of a loan would be that, more is incurred the longer the period taken to pay off the initial sum borrowed, and even more will be added on to the agreed sum should the schedule of payment in place is not strictly kept.

Therefore any defaults will incur penalties that are in most cases even harder to make payments on.

Although banks are the most popular avenues from which to seek out a loan from there are also other lending establishments that function sole for the purpose of facilitating loan arrangements.

Most of these are legal and with strict rules in place with proper accompanying documentation. However there are also loan facilities that can be gotten from "shady" sources which can sometimes be quite dangerous and definitely without the proper processes in place.

There are two very basic types of loans which are the secured one and the unsecured one.

The secured ones are based on some kind of acceptable collateral being offered in place of the loan which may include anything of value such as property, stocks, bond and others, and the unsecured one doesn't offer anything.

CHAPTER 2

BUSINESS LOANS

Synopsis

The basics of a business loan is very similar to that of other types of loans, which is the agreement struck between parties to lend a stipulated amount for a business where upon payment is returned with interest to the borrower over a fixed period of time.

For Business

These loans can be gotten from different sources of which banks are usually featured as the first choice as they generally do not own any part of the business and are just in the agreement to make money through the interest earned on the principal amount lent.

There are also equity investors, involving establishments or individuals who are willing to lend a sum of money in return for a vested interest in the business which usually comes in the form of shares in the said business.

The main differences between the two is that the former does not have any direct involvement in the business and only requires for the principal sum borrowed to be returned in full with interest paid over an agreed amount of time whereas the latter may sometimes incur the involvement of the lender and though no payment is required for the sum borrowed the lender now legally has a share in the business entity.

The promissory note is usually a document that is signed and witnessed in a legal setting whereby loan amounts, payment requirements, interest charged, time frames and any other agreed upon demands are clearly stated in the documentation.

The repayment of such promissory notes otherwise referred to as loans can be made in different methods which are also agreed upon at the onset of the process. These may include the following:

- Lump sum payments
- Periodic interest and lump sum repayment of principal
- Periodic payment of principal and interest
- Amortized payments
- Amortized payments with a balloon.

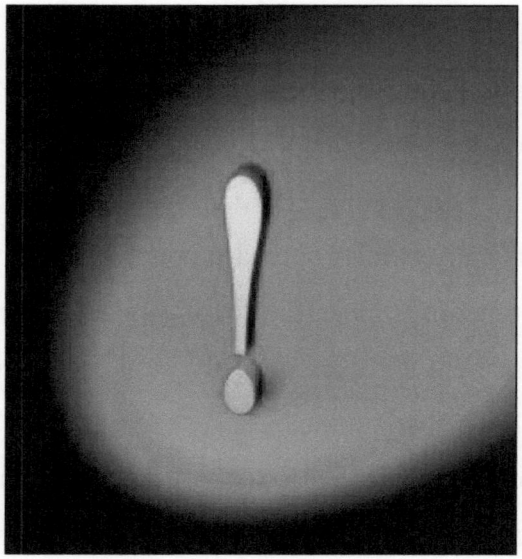

CHAPTER 3

USING COLLATERAL LOANS
FOR BUSINESS

Synopsis

Most business set ups often need the initial assistance of finance to get the business entity started. This is popularly acquired in the form of a loan which in most cases requires some sort of collateral to secure the intended loan amount more than adequately.

About Collateral

Most people turn to lending institutions such as banks, lending houses, finance houses and the likes for such assistance where some form of collateral is usually a designated requirement.

The process would require the lender to look over the company's history if any, business credit, revenues, balance sheets and equity contributions before an agreed sum can be settled upon.

When all this is in favorable condition then the next step would be for the borrower to provide collateral to secure the loan. The collateral is most commonly property, stocks, bonds and any other valuable assets the borrower may have that can equal or be more than the intended borrowed sum.

This would then be used to show the other possible source of loan repayment should there be a difficulty in servicing the repayments of the borrowed sum.

Keeping a detailed record of all the asset's worth is something that should be actively and accurately done every step of the way through the business setup.

Keeping such records will give those involved a better overview of the asset's worth and this can be done in a simple manner of an excel spreadsheet. The following are some things that can be used as collateral to secure a loan:

- Real property - still the most popular asset to be put up as collateral.

- Business inventory and accounts receivable – this is a little trickier but banks are usually willing to lend if there is clear evidence of an authenticated sizable order in the works.

- Cash savings and fixed deposits – personal assets that are tangible are more like to be favored by the lender as their risks are minimalized.

CHAPTER 4

USING PAYDAY LOANS/ CAR TITLE LOANS FOR BUSINESS

Synopsis

These are also other forms that can be used to secure loans for a business entity. These types of "collateral" are usually used only when there are smaller sums of money required by the borrower as the collateral put up in most cases in also small in comparison.

High Interest

Simply explained, the payday loan is effectively a type of advancement given to the individual seeking quick financial help for a short period of time.

The money lent would usually reflect a lesser than the amount to be received in the form of the payment for work rendered at the end of an agreed time frame.

This sort of borrowing and lending is usually done to cover expenses quickly and over a short period of time where the lengthy processes involved in getting a legitimate loan from licensed lending establishments would be inconveniencing and almost always unattainable.

This type of loan arrangement is usually classified as an unsecured loan by comparison. Ideally payment would be received in exchange for perhaps a post dated check which would include an interest amount calculated on the principal borrowed, and if by the collection date of the paycheck the borrowed is unable to make good on the agreed amount then the situation become complicated and nasty as the relevant machinery is put into different courses of action to recover what is due.

Car title loans are also another type of typically short term loan styles. In this scenario the car which is already paid for and considered a viable asset is put up as collateral for the intended loan amount.

The loan amount usually agreed upon is far less than the value of the car itself. Adding to this the interest charged for this type of loan is usually much higher than other types in the market as the risks involved are also usually higher. Although credit checks are done before the loans are approved these checks are rarely very stringent in nature.

CHAPTER 5

HOME EQUITY LOANS FOR BUSINESS

Synopsis

The home equity loan is another popular style often used for business purposes. Basically the home equity loan is a second mortgage taken out over an already existing one in which the property owner leverages the equity of their home against the borrowed amount.

Using Equity

The two main categories of the home equity loan would include the fixed rate loan and the line of credit loan. Both these are equally popular but usually chosen according the needs and compatibility of the borrower at the time monetary funds are an issue.

• The fixed rate loan provides a single, onetime payment to the borrower in which the repayment is done over a fixed period of time and at a fixed amount. The payment and interest does not change over the stipulated agreed upon period.

• Lines of credit style however differs in the basic dispersement of the borrowed amount. The initial amount is usually offered and agreed upon at the onset of the agreement; however the dispersement can be taken in amounts required at a particular time and for a particular amount. The monthly payments will vary depending on the amounts dispersed as the interests are only calculated on what has been utilized and not on the whole amount. However all outstanding amounts have to be repaid in full at the end of the due date of the agreement.

The home equity loan provides for a comparatively easy source of cash although the interest rates are higher than the first mortgage it is still a more viable way of acquiring cash resources quickly. It has been noted that besides using the money for business purposes the home equity lines of credit is also recommended to be a better option to use than credit cards advances as the interest rates incurred are far less in comparison. There are also better tax relief benefits in using the home equity loan option.

CHAPTER 6

THE IMPORTANCE OF MANAGING LOANS

Synopsis

The main reason and perhaps even the most important one for managing loans will is to ensure further penalties are not incurred due to negligence in payment requirements. This can and usually does happen when there are too many smaller debts that require the attention of the individual managing the debt collection exercise.

Important Points

In trying to minimize the possible occurrences of defaulting on payments, or not being able to make payments at the stipulated times and therefore incurring further interest on already outstanding amount one should consider consolidation the loans altogether.

Over time and statistically this has proven to be a better option to choose from as it not only facilitates lower interest rates by comparison it also is easier to manage when all loan payments are now less thus effectively converting it into one single payment.

Taking a serious view on managing debt is an important part of building a storm fiscal planning exercise. In keeping the debt manageable to the income ration the individual will be able to successfully work towards ideally eventually paying off the debt amount and plan towards saving for the future.

Not allowing the debt to spiral out of control should be the priority as it will eventually contribute to the individual being able to successfully pay down the accumulated debt without having to resort to more drastic measures.

Budgeting is important and getting a proper handle on one's personal monthly commitments and budgeting is an important first step in the right direction. Understanding and documenting what comes in and what goes out will help to get a clearer overview of the financial situation. It can also help to make adjustments where possible to being about better debt management. Establishing a strong and good credit platform is also important.

CHAPTER 7

STUDENT LOAN CONSOLIDATION: GETTING OUT OF DEBT

When we talk about college graduation, several promising life changes occur in our minds – potential careers, independence as well as new beginnings. However, although it means beginning of something, it still signifies something less enjoyable too – the repayment of student loans.

As you all know, the repayment of ample student loans can be off-putting for both students and their parents. It was found out by the Public Interest Research Group in the US that the average debt among student borrowers is currently in excess of $16,500. That large! The Associated Press also noted that graduates of public colleges and universities usually emerge owing more than $10,000 for their undergraduate years alone. Those who are in private institutions typically owe $14,000, while the graduate-level students often owe more than $24,000. What's more for those studying medicine or law? For sure, they accumulate even more debt. And, the bad thing is, repaying these debts are even becoming more difficult for graduates in the midst of uncertain jobs and the recession.

With the interest rates in all student loan programs are now at record lows, there is no reason for the graduates not to consider student loan consolidation. It is often said that with student loan consolidation, students and graduates can save thousands of bucks in interest charges.

Student loan consolidation is typically defined as the process or the act of combining multiple loans into a single loan in order to decrease the monthly payment amount or elevate the repayment period. There are a lot of reasons behind it, and among those is money saving payment incentives, decreased monthly payments, fixed interest rates, and new or renewed deferments.

The Plus Factors of Consolidation

Student loan consolidation has a lot to offer. That is what many experts often say. To find out what consolidation has to offer, let's read on.

Overall Interest Savings

Over time, the student loans you have borrowed have been assigned with different variable interest rates. Note that the key word here is *variable*. While the loan you received may have offered, say, 3.5 percent at first, the rate will actually go up as the interest rates go up. So, if you have two or more of these loans, there is a great possibility that you may have owed amounts at different rates, and these rates can rise and fall yearly. Considering that the interest rates have nowhere else to go but up, it is no doubt a safe bet that the debt you have accumulated will mount faster than it would if you consider a student loan consolidation.

By considering consolidation and remaining on your 10 years payment plan, it is possible that you can lock your interest at today's current loan rates and save some bucks over the long haul. Aside from that, all of those loans that may have come from different lending companies or banks can be a burden to deal with. So, if you consolidate, it means that you only deal with one single company and one payment rather than several. Other than that, you have the great chance to receive added bonuses like payment and interest rate reductions in case you pay your debts on time over a period of months. These benefits are also possible to come if you have automatically withdrawn your monthly payment from a checking or savings account.

Improved Credit Score

By considering a loan consolidation, borrowers not only save or reduce their long term debt but can also help change their credit score for the better over time. It is worth noting that an improved credit score is a very important factor when a person enters the "real" world and wants a new car, apartment or charge card.

Here are some tips for you that can help you as you enter the job market.

• *More Open Accounts, The Lower the Score:* Over the student borrower's life, he or she may have borrowed up to eight separate loans to pay for school. Each of these loans has a different payback amount, payment terms and interest rate. The more accounts the student has opened, the lower the over credit score. Thereby, lowering the amount of open credit lines on a credit report is needed, but this can only be made possible through a student loan consolidation in which the older accounts will be combined into a single account.

- *The Lower the Payments, the Higher the Score:* When the credit report evaluation comes, it is usual in the process that the amount of the borrower's monthly minimum payments is taken into account. So, when you hold a number of loans, every payment is considered part of the borrower's monthly payment obligation. Those who have considered consolidation have only one payment to make, which is typically lower than the minimum amount of the separate, multiple loans.

- *The Debt to Credit Ratio Matters:* As you may know, the credit bureaus typically find out if you are in debt. They do this by way of evaluating the amount of your available credit you actually use. So, in case you have a total of $10,000 available on three credit lines and you owe $2,000, your score will then be considered higher than especially if you have maxed out your on credit line with a $2,000 limit. It is worthy to note that if a person has several loans with a maximum used, it will reflect negatively on his or her credit score. Given this fact, consolidating the accounts is very important in order to lessen the number of open accounts being used.

Returning to School is a Possibility

Many students and graduates left school for family, career or financial reasons. The odds here are they will want to return to college down the line. However, if they fail to pay on their student loans while they are out of school, there is a great possibility that they can be kept from receiving any financial aid when they return. So, if financial reasons were part of the primary reason they left school, it therefore implies that digging a much deeper hole will only make it harder for them to come back.

By consolidating, the loans will also become easier to manage and pay off. And, once the loans are consolidated, you can retain your right for forbearance as well as for deferment. You can even take advantage of income sensitive and graduate repayment options which you may not have encountered before while you're on your multiple loans.

Hiding from Loans is Impossible

There is one particular truth when it comes to student loans – you can't hide from them. It may sound extreme though, but school loans are completely immune to bankruptcy and those students or graduates that failed to pay their bills face stiff punishments. The usual consequences are poor credit ratings, garnishment of wages, and IRS penalties.

Besides, attaining licenses in certain fields is impossible when you failed to pay off your student loan debts. There is even a chance that you may be excluded from some government contracts if you own a small business. With all these consequences, it is then clear that avoiding a student loan is no way to start a life after college. If you do come back and take out more and more student loans, you will be able to consolidate again after graduation.

In the end, about half of the students coming out of college have actually gained their degrees. Of course, it can be tough to remain and stay in school with financial burdens, and it is harder to come back. But, thanks to student loan consolidation that creating one less barrier to coming back to school and keeping your credit rating clean is now possible.

The Right Period to Consolidate

In the government consolidation loan program, it is interesting to know that there are actually no deadlines connected to it. It is supported by the fact that you can apply for the student loan anytime during the grace period or even on the repayment period. But to consolidate student loans, some considerations must be paid attention. To consolidate student loans, you should know that it usually take place during your grace period. At this moment, the lower in-school interest rate will then be applied to estimate the weighted average fixed rate to consolidate student loans. And once the grace period has ended on your government student loans, the higher in-repayment interest rate will be applied to estimate the weighted average fixed rate. Given such process, it is then understandable that your fixed interest rate for government student loan consolidation will be higher if you consolidate student loans after your grace period.

And when you are interested to consolidate student loans, you should know that even of your student loans are already in repayment, to consolidate student loans is still allowed and beneficial. It is for the reason that when you consolidate student loans at this time, you already fix the interest rate on your government student loans while the rates are still originally low.

As presented, student loan consolidation can help most borrowers in many ways. But, it is still necessary to note that rates won't actually stay low without end. In fact, they are so low now and the only place for rates to go is up. So, if you are on your way out of college, saving every cent you can in today's tough job market is worth considering. And, regardless of the situation you are in to right now, consolidating your college loans is a practical decision.

CHAPTER 8

STUDENT LOAN PITFALLS: DANGEROUS DEFAULT

The student loans just like the other forms of financial aid are a service that is subject for repayment. However, although aware of such fact, many borrowers still fall to the trap of walking away from student loan debt which then results to series of consequences. They tend to ignore their being summoned to enter repayment usually either 90 or 120 days after separating from school or after dropping below half-time enrollment. With this, the loans remain delinquent for 270 days or become 270 days past due at any time, leading the loans to "default" status.

Student Loan Default, Defined

Defaulted student loans are actually defaults made by the borrower to the creditor of the terms and conditions of the student loan contract. It is usually caused by the act of escaping from debts, leading to unfavorable consequences on the part of the borrower.

Basically, prior to the declaration of student loan default is the delinquency period. At this period, the lenders of student loans authorized under Title IV of the Higher Education Act will exhaust all efforts to find and contact the borrower. If the lender's efforts of locating the debtor are unsuccessful, the loan will then be placed in default. It will be turned over to either the state guaranty agency or the Department of Education. And, once the loan enters the default status, the maturity date is accelerated, making the overall payment in full due right away.

The Consequences of Student Loan Default

When the loan enters the default status, several consequences are connected to it. Some of them are mentioned below:

- The loans may be turned over to a collection agency.

- The borrower will be liable for all the costs associated with collecting the loan. This may even include the court costs as well as attorney fees.

- The borrower can be sued for the entire amount of the loan.

- The wages may be garnished.

- The federal and state income tax refunds may be intercepted.

- That federal government may withhold part of the Social Security benefit payments.

- On the credit record, the defaulted loans will be mentioned, making it difficult for the borrower to get an auto loan, mortgage and even credit cards. Note that having a bad credit record can harm your ability to find a job.

- The borrower's chance to receive federal financial aid will now be impossible to happen until he repays the loan in full or make arrangements to repay what he already owe and make at least six consecutive, on time, monthly payments.

- Federal interest benefits will be denied.

Aside from the above mentioned consequences, there is also some other less- obvious consequences that are oftentimes omitted from consideration. One of those could be the rule that the federal student loan borrowers holding defaulted student loans are no longer entitled to any deferments or forbearances. Subsequently, there are some instances when the loan default may force the individual to consider or take a semester off. This must be taken due to his or her inability to qualify for federal student aid as well as to afford the cost of higher education independently.

What's more, there is a great possibility for those borrowers who defaulted on their student loans to lose their professional licenses. For instance, the lawyers who possess defaulted loans may be subject to have their license to practice law disavowed. The doctors and certified public accountants would also fall into this category.

Lastly, the borrowers who just ignored summons for loan repayments will become liable for all fees associated with collecting the federally financed loan. This means that the borrowers will end up repaying their outstanding debt, plus up to 25 percent in contingent fees in order to satisfy the student loan debt. Note that this rule is actually consistent with the Higher Education Act as well as on the terms of most borrowers' promissory notes.

The Collection Procedures Involved with Defaulted Student Loans

Most of the guaranty agencies' stringent collection procedures have successfully deterred student loan neglect. One of the supports for this claim is the steady decrease and current all-time low of student loan default rates. However, although the collections department is highly committed to assisting those who are in default and making repayment as simple as possible, the non-response in the borrowers' side still opens up to one or more of the following collection approaches:

- ***Garnishment of Administrative Wage:*** Under the Higher Education Act of 1965, the Department of Education as well as the state guaranty agencies may require employers who employ individuals with defaulted student loans to take away 10 to 15 percent of the debtor's disposable income per pay period. The garnishment of the administrative wage is actually a resort taken only when the debtor refuses to voluntarily repay his or her defaulted debts and may persist until the total balance of the outstanding debt is paid back.

- ***Treasury Offset Payments:*** Aside from administrative wage garnishment, the Department of Education has the right to request the Treasury Department to perform a federal offset against the federal income tax refunds as a way of collecting defaulted student loan debt. To simply put, the borrowers with loans in default status may forgo any federal tax refunds until he or she has repaid the defaulted loan.

- *Legal Action:* Litigation can be pursued by the Department of Education as well as state guaranty agencies as a means for collecting the defaulted loans. It means that if the debtor refuses to repay the debt voluntarily, he or she is subject to prosecution in a state or federal district court. The borrower is therefore sued for the outstanding debt as well as for the attorney and court fees. But, these methods are usually considered as last resorts, thus need prior notice of the proposed offset.

Preventing Default

There are several ways that you can make to prevent the onset of student loan default. It is just somehow necessary for you to place your interest and efforts on preventing it. Here are the possible ways that you can consider:

1. Make sure that you understand your loan options as well as the related responsibilities prior to taking out a student loan.

2. Simply make your payments on time.

3. If possible, inform your lender or service provider promptly about any of the possible adjustments that may affect the repayment of your student loan. In case you move or change your address, let them know. Also, make sure that they know about the name changes, which are very possible because of marriage; graduation or termination of studies; leaves of absence as well as transfers to another institution.

4. If certain financial difficulties are encountered, try to consider applying for a deferment or forbearance on your loans. Many experts often suggest that it is much better to defer your payments than to go in to default status. Along with this, ask your lender or service provider about the available options while you are still making payments, before you enter the default status of your loan. Always note that after you default, you won't be able to get a deferment or forbearance anymore.

5. If for instance you are having trouble making your payments, try to contact your lender as they may be able to suggest an alternate repayment options for you. Some of the possible options include graduated repayment, income sensitive repayment, as well as income contingent repayment. Also note that the types of available repayment options currently depend on whether the student loan was issued under the FFELP or FDSLP or Direct student loan programs.

6. A student loan consolidation can be considered as another way for preventing student loan default. Combine all of your educational loans into one big loan as this gives you the chance to send your payments to just one lender. What's more, you may be able to extend the term of the loan in order to lessen the size of your monthly payments.

7. Simply keep records regarding your student loans. If possible, try to back up copies of all your letters, canceled checks, promissory notes, disbursement notices, and some other necessary forms in a file folder. Just be organized.

Getting Out of Default

In case your loan already entered the default status, don't worry. You still have hopes if you will just try to pay even just a little consideration on your debts. The first move to take to get out of debt is simply to make arrangements with your lender to repay the loan. It is commonly noted that once you have made six regular payments, there is a chance for you to be eligible for an additional Title IV aid. After you have completed twelve regular payments and applied for and received "rehabilitation", you will no longer be considered in default. It is also at this time when the record of the default will be eliminated from the reports to credit reporting bureaus.

And, for further information about the available repayment options that could suit your needs, just contact your lender. The financial aid office at your school should also be able to tell you the name, address as well as the contact number of your lender. They can also give you supporting help and advice about your repayment problems.

Student Loan Rehabilitation

As the phrase suggests, the loan rehabilitation is a program designed to rehabilitate the defaulted student loans and return such loans to a favorable status. This program actually requires 12 consecutive monthly payments of a predetermined agreeable amount.

It is often suggested that those borrowers in default status must contact their servicing agency to define the loan rehabilitation program that is reasonable to both parties. However, if a reasonable rehabilitation program cannot be reached with your lender, there is the office of the Federal Student Aid Ombudsman, which is a neutral party, designed to resolve any disputes.

Having said all these, the defaulted student loans are no doubt a serious problem that must be healed as soon as possible. This is for the fact that when the case intensifies, certain damages not only on the person's credit rating, but other consequences as mentioned above will greatly result like a brush of fire.

Wrapping Up

Being in the know of the current overall financial market sentiments of the time will also allow the individual to make better financial commitments which are in his or her favor.

Printed by Libri Plureos GmbH in Hamburg,
Germany